CLEARLY MATH

GRADE 2

Written by Robyn Silbey

Illustrated by Sherry Neidigh

Editor: Stephanie Garcia
Copy Editors: Michael Batty, Robert Newman
Book Design: Anthony D. Paular
Graphic Artist: Daniel Willits
J331002 Clearly Math Grade 2

TABLE OF CONTENTS

INTRODUCTION

Clearly Math is designed to help students develop a deep understanding of basic math concepts taught in second grade. Focus areas of study complement the <u>NCTM Principles and Standards for School Mathematics</u> (PSSM). *Clearly Math* encourages students to think creatively and critically. Questions are provided, both in activities and on the reproducibles, that can be used as springboards for rich classroom discussions. The activities in *Clearly Math* help students apply their skills and knowledge in a variety of formats and presentations.

Clearly Math content areas of study are separated into six strands. Each strand features hands-on, minds-on concept-building activities as well as several reproducibles. As an added bonus, *Clearly Math* features a collection of *full-color transparencies* for use throughout the book. A special box near the title of the activity or on the reproducible page tells you that a transparency is recommended for best results. Place the transparency on an overhead projector and present the activity or reproducible to your students. You are all set for a successful lesson that requires little preparation time for you.

Finally, *Clearly Math* contains assessment activities that evaluate conceptual understanding. These activities, labeled Assessing Conceptual Understanding (ACU) appear in each unit and can be evaluated using the rubric below.

Clearly Math can be used all year to captivate students and enrich math instruction.

Tips for Using the Transparency Pages

These transparency pages include interdisciplinary connections and teaching aids. Here are some tips on how to use and store them:

1. The transparencies may be duplicated for use by individual students or groups of students when completing some of the activities in this book. The full-color feature of the transparencies will add interest to the activities when used on an overhead projector. The colors will become gray when photocopied, but the pages will still be usable by the students.

2. Some of the transparencies are meant to be cut apart and used as manipulatives on the overhead projector. It is recommended that you make photocopies before cutting transparencies apart, to be kept with the pieces.

3. You may wish to store your transparencies in envelopes. Add holes to the envelopes with a three-hole punch, put the pieces in the envelopes, and put the envelopes in a binder. Be sure to label each envelope.

RUBRIC FOR ASSESSING CONCEPTUAL UNDERSTANDING ACU ACTIVITIES

3 The child's performance or work sample shows a thorough understanding of the topic. Work is clearly explained with examples and/or words, all calculations are correct, and explanations reflect reasoning beyond the simplicity of the calculations.

2 The child's performance or work sample shows a good understanding of the topic. There may be some errors in calculations, but the work reflects a general knowledge of details and a reasonable understanding of mathematical ideas.

1 The child's performance or work sample shows a limited understanding of the topic. The written work does not reflect understanding of the problem, and examples contain errors.

0 The child's performance or work sample is too weak to evaluate or is nonexistent.

Number Patterns with Tens and Hundreds

In this activity, the children will construct groups of 100 with collections of tens.

1. Provide each pair of children with a collection of 10 tens blocks, or longs, and 1 hundreds block, or flat.

2. Have each pair stack the tens blocks on top of the hundreds block to discover how many tens make one hundred (10).

3. Ask the pairs to separate the tens to make two groups that would be combined to make 100. For example, the children may separate the tens into groups of three and seven.

4. Have the children say the number sentences that the blocks show. If they showed three tens and seven tens, for example, the children would write $30 + 70 = 100$.

5. If time and interest permit, have the children separate their blocks to make three groups with corresponding number sentences such as $30 + 40 + 30 = 100$.

As an extension, repeat this activity with hundreds blocks to make one thousand. The children may, for example, use the hundreds blocks, or flats, and thousands blocks, or cubes, to find that $300 + 700 = 1,000$.

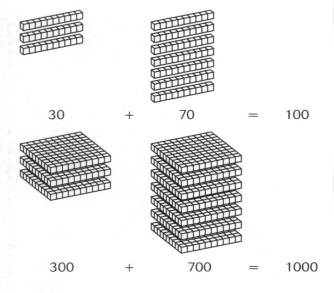

| 30 | + | 70 | = | 100 |

| 300 | + | 700 | = | 1000 |

"Connecting" Tens and Ones

Transparency 1

Have children use dimes and pennies to model two-digit numbers.

1. Display the *Hundred Chart* transparency and provide the children with copies. Distribute collections of dimes and pennies to the children at their desks or tables.

2. Write an amount in cents on the chalkboard, such as 36¢. Ask the children how many dimes (3) and pennies (6) they need to make the amount.

3. Demonstrate on the overhead and have the children place dimes on the 10, 20, and 30 squares; and pennies on the squares numbered 31 through 36.

4. When the children have placed all of their coins on their charts, have them read the numbered squares with you: "10, 20, 30, 31, 32, 33, 34, 35, 36."

5. Repeat the procedure for several other two-digit numbers to demonstrate the relationship between tens and ones and dimes and pennies.

Three-Clue Riddles

Reading number riddles to children helps them to listen and to relate the numbers that they hear with the numbers that they read and write.

1. Pose riddles such as the following for the children to solve:

   I have four hundreds.

   I have one more ten than I have hundreds.

   I have eight ones.

   Which number am I? (458)

2. After you write several riddles, invite the children to write their own. Check the accuracy of their riddles. Solutions should correspond to the number of ones, tens, and hundreds suggested by the riddles. After their riddles have been checked, allow the children time to solve one another's riddles.

Number Order

Transparency 1

Children can compare two-digit numbers easily when they use a hundred chart.

1. Display the *Hundred Chart* transparency on the overhead projector.

2. Have two volunteers use overhead counters to identify a pair of random numbers on the chart, such as 38 and 51.

3. Invite the children to "vote," using thumbs-up or thumbs-down to show which number they think is greater. Call out the two numbers and count votes.

4. Repeat Steps 2 and 3 several times. Ask the children to think about the position of the counter showing the greater number relative to the counter showing the lesser number (always closer to the 100th square or to the right end of the number line).

5. When the children can find the greater number easily, repeat the activity, but this time have them find the lesser number.

Number Line Patterns for Tens and Hundreds

Transparency 2

This activity helps children think critically about patterns and missing numbers in a sequence.

1. Display the number line showing 0–100 with multiples of ten from the *Number Lines* transparency. You may wish to cover the remaining number lines with a sheet of paper so the children can focus on this line.

2. Have the children count aloud by tens from 0 to 100 as you point to the numbers. Repeat several times.

3. Next, ask the children to cover their eyes. Use ones cubes to conceal some of the numbers on the number line. Ask the children to open their eyes and challenge them to identify which numbers are concealed.

4. Ask volunteers to come to the front of the room and repeat the activity, concealing numbers and challenging classmates to identify them.

5. Distribute reproduced copies of the number lines. Have the children work in pairs and repeat the activity.

6. Repeat this activity for hundreds, using the number line 0–1,000.

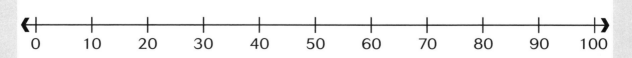

Block and Roll

In this game, children will model and order three-digit numbers. After a while, they'll begin to develop their own strategies to help them win the game!

1. Supply pairs of children with sets of three dice and base-ten blocks of hundreds, tens, and ones.

2. Have the partners take turns rolling the number cubes and modeling the greatest numbers that they can with the results. For example, a child should model a roll of 1, 2, and 3 as 321.

3. Have the partners compare their models and write two number sentences showing the comparison. For example, children comparing 321 and 432 may write 321 < 432 and 432 > 321.

4. The child with the greater number scores one point. Have the children repeat Steps 2 and 3. The child who scores five points first wins the game.

5. After the children have finished playing the game, ask them to write paragraphs, describing their strategies for finding the greatest number for each given roll, using examples if they like. (The children should mention that they order the numbers greatest to least in the greatest to least place values. In other words, for a roll of 1, 2, and 3, the child should put 3 in the hundreds place since it is the greatest number and hundreds is the place with greatest value.)

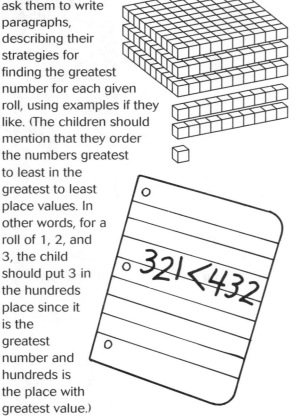

Make a Pattern

In this activity, children will make their own patterns with series of three-digit numbers.

1. Write the number 345 on the chalkboard. Following it, write 346, 347, and 348. Ask the children to name the next three numbers in the pattern and describe how they know (349, 350, 351; the numbers increase by 1 each time).

2. Begin with 345 again. This time, write 355, 365, and 375. Ask the children to name the next three numbers and explain how they arrived at their predictions (385, 395, 405; the numbers increase by 10 each time).

3. Begin with 345 and write 445 and 555. Repeat the questioning as in Steps 1 and 2 (655, 755, 855; the numbers increase by 100 each time).

4. Begin with a different number and repeat the activity.

5. After the children can easily identify and continue these patterns, try the following variations:

   a. Write numbers that increase by increments of 2, 20, or 200 or some other multiple of 1, 10, and 100.

   b. Write numbers that decrease by increments of 1, 10, 100, or some multiple thereof.

Post Office Place Value

Use the color key to color.

2 in the ones place	red	2 in the tens place	green
3 in the ones place	orange	4 in the tens place	blue
9 in the ones place	yellow	8 in the tens place	purple

Name _____

The "Greatest" Code

Circle the letter below the greatest number.

1.	45 R	65 S	41 T	2.	37 G	52 H	25 I
3.	76 E	67 F	66 G	4.	21 G	12 H	19 I
5.	91 O	90 P	89 Q	6.	28 C	21 D	30 E
7.	50 S	45 T	48 U	8.	82 R	78 S	87 T
9.	35 M	37 N	41 O	10.	60 R	63 S	59 T
11.	90 W	88 X	79 Y	12.	21 D	31 E	29 F
13.	39 D	41 E	40 F	14.	45 O	50 P	48 Q

What does a broom do at night?

To find out, write the letter you circled above each number.

___ ___ ___   ___ ___ ___ ___
 1   2   3   4   5   6   7

___ ___   ___ ___ ___ ___ ___
 8   9   10 11 12 13 14

J331002 Clearly Math • Grade 2

Cross-Number Puzzle

Use the clues to complete the puzzle.

Across

A. Three hundred twenty-six

B. Two hundred five

D. Two hundred seventy-eight

F. Nine hundred thirty-seven

G. Seven hundred twenty-nine

I. Five hundred sixty-six

K. Eight hundred twelve

L. Four hundred

Down

A. Three hundred ninety-two

C. Five hundred forty-seven

E. Eight hundred nineteen

F. Nine hundred seventy-five

H. Two hundred thirty-one

J. Six hundred ninety

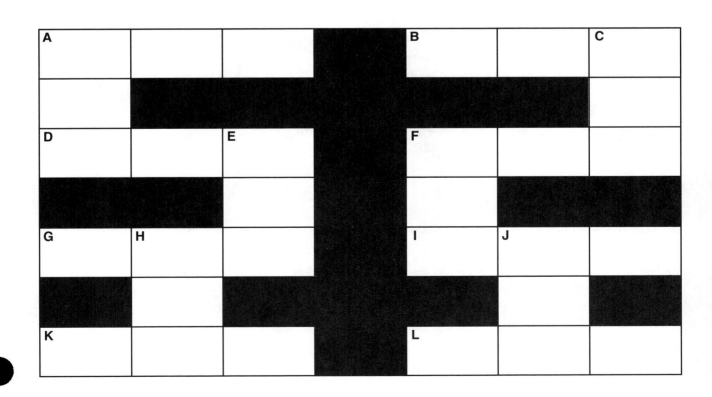

Name _____

Make It True

Complete each sentence with < or > to make it true.

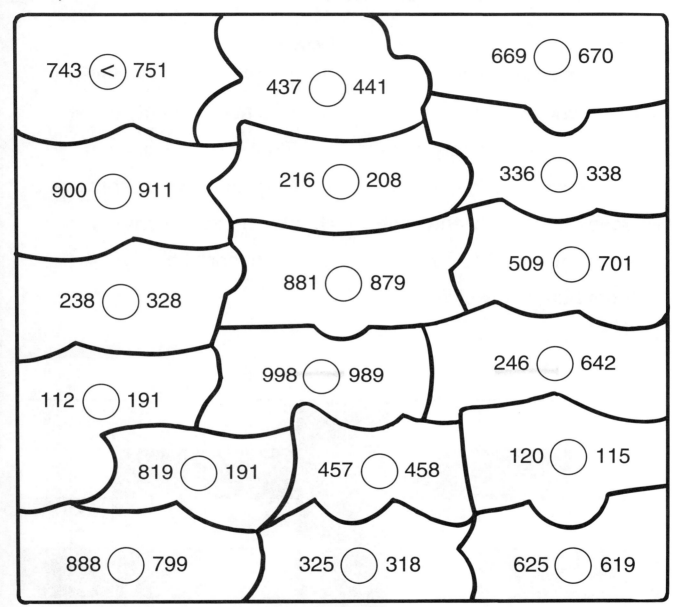

743 $<$ 751

437 ◯ 441

669 ◯ 670

900 ◯ 911

216 ◯ 208

336 ◯ 338

238 ◯ 328

881 ◯ 879

509 ◯ 701

112 ◯ 191

998 ◯ 989

246 ◯ 642

819 ◯ 191

457 ◯ 458

120 ◯ 115

888 ◯ 799

325 ◯ 318

625 ◯ 619

Color each < shape yellow. Color each > shape orange.

Write < or > to make the following sentence true.

Yellow shapes ◯ orange shapes

Point in the Right Direction

Draw arrows to show the numbers from least to greatest. Circle the greatest number in each group. The first one has been done for you.

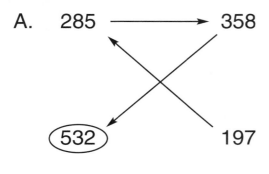

A. 285 ⟶ 358

(532)   197

B. 852   241

405   617

C. 927   319

530   619

D. 456   654

546   555

E. 498   416

429   501

F. 327   273

295   308

G. 780   779

817   821

H. 514   541

520   511

ADDITION

Connections: Regrouping with Cubes

Transparency 3

In this activity, children will construct and regroup tens.

1. Provide each pair of children with two number cubes (or dice), a photocopy of the *Place Value Mat* transparency (page 59), and nine ten-trains of connecting cubes.

2. Have a child in each pair roll the number cubes. Then have the child use the numerals rolled to model the smallest number he or she can with the connecting cubes. For example, a roll of 5 and 1 should be modeled as the number 15.

3. Have children in each pair place the modeled number on the tens and ones workmat.

4. Have the two children combine the ones and see if they can make a ten-train. If they can, they should move the ten-train to the tens section of the workmat. If they can't, the cubes should stay in the ones section.

5. Have the pair count the ones and tens to find the sum of the two rolled numbers.

6. Have each pair of children repeat the process several times to reinforce the concept of regrouping.

Toy Time

Transparency 4

In this simple critical thinking activity, children must use estimation and guess-and-check to budget and buy what they like. Begin by displaying the *Toy Treasures* transparency.

1. Tell the children to imagine that they have $1.00.

2. Have each child make a list of items that he or she would like to buy with his or her money. Provide the following guidelines:

   • Each child may buy more than one of any item.

   • Each child should spend as close to $1.00 (without going over) as he or she can.

3. Ask the children to show their calculations. In addition, have the children write or tell you how they arrived at their solutions. Accept all responses with total token expenses between $0.90 and $1.00. Explanations will vary, but responses should indicate some use of estimation, logical reasoning, and addition strategies.

4. You may wish to extend this activity by challenging the children to spend up to $3.00. Accept responses between $2.75 and $3.00.

Game: Race to 100

This game offers ample opportunities to practice regrouping.

1. Provide each pair of children with a number cube (or die) and 1 hundreds block, along with a collection of tens blocks and ones blocks.

2. Player A should roll the number cube and take that many ones. Player B should do the same.

3. Player A should roll again and take the number of ones shown. If Player A has accumulated 10 ones, he or she should trade them in for a tens block. Player B should do the same.

4. Players should continue to take turns. After each roll, each player should trade in 10 ones blocks for a tens block, if possible.

5. Play continues until one player in each pair can trade in 10 tens blocks for 1 hundred block. He or she then wins the game.

Mental Math with the Hundred Chart

Children will learn how to combine addends like 27 + 19 mentally by using the *Hundred Chart* transparency.

1. Display the *Hundred Chart* transparency. Have the children locate the square numbered 27.

2. Challenge the children to figure out how to add 19 to 27 on the hundred chart. If necessary, guide the children by suggesting that they locate the square that is 20 greater than 27 by counting down two squares (47). Then have the children locate the square marked with a number one less than 47 (46).

3. Help the children realize that to add 19 mentally, they can add 20 and then subtract 1.

4. Repeat with several examples, such as 39 + 19 (58), 45 + 19 (64), and 18 + 19 (37).

5. When the children understand the concept, extend the activity and have children use the hundred square to add 53 + 29 (82), 27 + 39 (66), 41 + 19 (60), and so on.

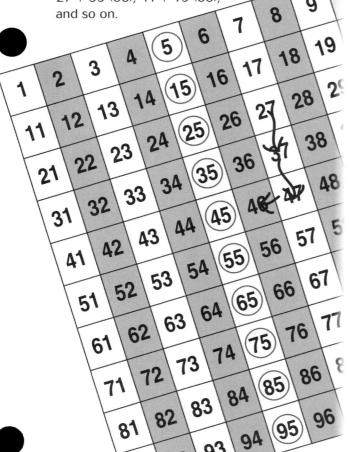

Three-Digit Block Sums

1. Supply pairs of children with collections of hundreds, tens, and ones blocks and copies of the *Place Value Mat* transparency.

2. Write *234 + 593* on the chalkboard. Have each pair of children model both numbers on one workmat.

3. Have the children combine the ones and find the total (7).

4. As the children combine the tens blocks, remind them that they can exchange 10 of them for 1 hundreds block. If necessary, have the children "prove" that 10 tens blocks is equal to 1 hundreds block.

5. After the regrouping is complete, have each pair of children add the hundreds, tens, and ones. Ask the children to tell the sum (827).

6. Repeat the procedure with several different pairs of addends to reinforce the concept of regrouping.

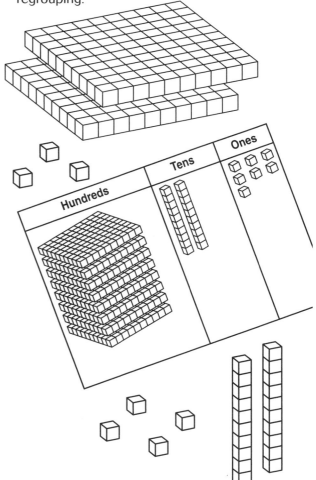

Magic Squares

Add across and down. Find each magic square sum. The first one has been started for you.

A.

5	2	7
3	1	
8		◯

B.

6	0	
7	2	
		◯

C.

4	8	
3	1	
		◯

D.

3	5	
3	6	
		◯

E.

1	9	
4	3	
		◯

F.

2	1	
7	8	
		◯

Hunt for Sums

Follow the clues. Draw an arrow to show the next box on the path. Your arrows should touch all boxes.

START

| Here is 56. Find the sum of 72 and 19. | Here is 91. Find the sum of 45 and 27. | Here is 48. Find the sum of 32 and 26. |

| | Here is 72. Find the sum of 19 and 29. | Here is 58. Find the sum of 37 and 37. |

| Here is 99. Find the sum of 28 and 28. | Here is 74. Find the sum of 46 and 25. | Here is 71. Find the sum of 26 and 68. |

| Here is 95. Find the sum of 33 and 66. | Here is 94. Find the sum of 31 and 59. | Here is 90. Find the sum of 23 and 56. |

| Here is 88. Find the sum of 49 and 46. | Here is 79. Find the sum of 41 and 51. | Here is 92. Find the sum of 9 and 69. |

| Here is 70. Find the sum of 39 and 49. | Here is 57. Find the sum of 58 and 12. | Here is 78. Find the sum of 26 and 31. |

Name _____

Choose Three

Three numbers make each given sum.
Cross out the number that you do not need.
Add the other three numbers. Show your work in the box.

A. Sum: 83

   19 20 34 44

B. Sum: 72

   14 23 25 33

C. Sum: 68

   12 14 26 28

D. Sum: 80

   12 19 37 49

E. Sum: 88

   17 28 38 43

F. Sum: 93

   26 32 35 41

G. Sum: 70

   11 13 24 35

H. Sum: 98

   19 23 38 41

Buy a Toy

Use the *Toy Treasures* transparency to solve each problem. Show your work.

A. Reena got a beaded bracelet and a beaded necklace. How much did she spend?

_____

B. Jana got two toy motorcycles. How much did she spend?

_____

C. Ira got a toy car and a toy truck. How much did he spend?

_____

D. Ron got one small and one large stuffed animal. How much did he spend?

_____

E. Grace wants 2 plastic spiders and a toy truck. How much does she need?

_____

F. Josh wants a small stuffed animal, a toy motorcycle, and a toy car. How much does he need?

_____

G. Todd has 56¢. Jeff gives him 15¢. Does Todd have enough money to buy a large stuffed animal? Explain.

_____

H. Gayla has 25¢. Hannah gives her 12¢. Does Gayla have enough money to buy a toy car? Explain.

_____

I. Choose two or three toys that you would like to buy. Find out how much money you will need.

_____

Name _____

Sum Search

Add. Shade each sum in the box
at the bottom of the page.

A.   400   275   619   82   918
     + 300   + 314   + 145   + 147   + 20

B.   256   529   791   359   272
     + 336   + 57   + 144   + 135   + 460

C.   333   282   92   326   286
     + 586   + 352   + 462   + 428   + 103

D.   473   542   307   499   423
     + 355   + 173   + 209   + 215   + 329

700	123	589	456	754	721	938
494	189	919	314	752	592	935
516	517	186	442	715	487	634
554	201	732	322	714	101	828
764	897	586	789	389	915	229

The secret word is _____ .

Multiplication Match

Match each problem to a group of shapes. The first one has been done for you.

3 + 3 + 3 + 3 - - - - - - - - - - - - - - - - -   2 x 9

5 + 5 + 5   4 x 3

9 + 9   5 x 4

4 + 4 + 4 + 4 + 4   3 x 5

6 + 6 + 6   3 x 7

8 + 8   4 x 2

7 + 7 + 7   3 x 6

2 + 2 + 2 + 2   2 x 8

SUBTRACTION

Fact Families

ACU

Children will extend their understanding of the relationship between addition and subtraction by making fact families with greater numbers.

1. Have the children review the meaning of fact families. Ask volunteers to name fact families that they know. Examples will vary but may include $9 + 6 = 15$, $6 + 9 = 15$, $15 - 9 = 6$, $15 - 6 = 9$. Ask the children to think about whether or not a fact family can be made from numbers of any size.

2. Direct each child to choose any 2 two-digit numbers. Ask the children to do the following on paper:

   a. Find the sum of the numbers.

   b. Change the order of the numbers. Find the sum again.

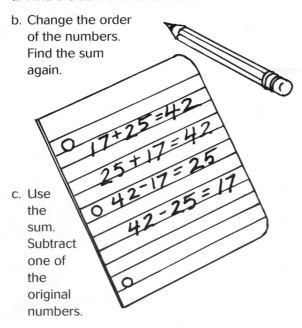

   c. Use the sum. Subtract one of the original numbers.

   d. Use the sum. Subtract the other original number.

3. Beneath the four examples, have the children write responses to the question: "Can a fact family be made from numbers of any size? Why or why not?" (Children may say that order does not change the sum in an addition sentence, and that when one part of a sum is removed, the result is the other part. They may also say that addition and subtraction are inverse operations, or that subtraction can "undo" addition.)

Connections: Regrouping with Cubes

Transparency 3

In this activity, children will break apart ten-trains as they model regrouping.

1. Have the children work in pairs. Provide each pair with two number cubes labeled with numerals 1–6, one spinner labeled 7–9, a photocopy of the *Place Value Mat* transparency on page 59, and 9 ten-trains of connecting cubes.

2. One child in each pair should roll the number cubes. Then the child should use the numerals rolled to model the greatest number he or she can with the connecting cubes. For example, a roll of 3 and 4 would result in modeling 43 on the workmat.

3. The child's partner should spin to determine how many ones will be removed from the modeled number. If a 7 is spun, for example, 7 cubes would be removed from 43. In order to make more ones, each pair of children should separate 1 ten-train into 10 single cubes and put them in the ones place on the workmat.

4. The children should count the remaining cubes to find the difference.

5. Have the pairs of children repeat the process several times to reinforce the concept of regrouping. As they become more comfortable, have the children write corresponding number sentences. For the example above, children would write $43 - 7 = 36$.

6. As an extension, have both children in each pair roll the number cubes. The greater number that can be made from the numerals rolled should be placed on the mat, and the lesser number should be subtracted, or removed. Children can follow the steps outlined above.

Game: Race to Erase

This game offers ample opportunities to practice regrouping.

1. Have the children work in pairs. Provide each pair with a number cube and a hundreds block, along with a collection of tens blocks and ones blocks.

2. Player A should roll the number cube and remove that many ones. In order to do this, he or she must regroup the hundreds block as 10 tens blocks, then regroup 1 tens block as 10 ones blocks. When the regrouping is complete, Player A should remove the ones.

3. Player B should repeat the process in Step 2.

4. Player A should roll again and remove the number of ones shown. If regrouping is needed, he or she should regroup another tens block as 10 ones blocks. Player B should do the same.

5. Players should continue to take turns. Regrouping should occur as needed.

6. Play continues until a player runs out of blocks and wins the game.

More Mental Math

Children will learn how to subtract 9 from 46 mentally with the *Hundred Chart* transparency.

1. Display the *Hundred Chart* transparency. Have the children locate the square numbered 46.

2. Challenge the children to figure out how to subtract 9 from 46 on the hundred chart. If necessary, suggest that they locate the square with a number that is 10 less than 46 by moving up one square (36). Then have the children locate the square with a number that is one more than 36 (37).

3. Repeat the process several times, having children subtract 9 from 43 (34), 65 (56), and 92 (83). Help the children realize that to subtract 9 mentally, they can subtract 10 and then add 1.

4. After the children are familiar with this concept, have them subtract 19 from several numbers, such as 67 (48), 81 (62), and 48 (29).

5. As an extension, have the children make up their own problems and challenge classmates to use mental math and the hundred chart to solve.

Checking Subtraction with Addition

In this game, children will use addition to check subtraction problems written by classmates.

1. Have the children work in small groups. Provide each group with three index cards, a paper bag, and a plain sheet of paper.

2. On the plain sheet of paper, have each group write a subtraction problem and solve it.

3. Have each group write the three numbers that make up the problem on three separate index cards. Have the children put the index cards and the sheet of paper into the bag.

4. Have groups exchange bags with each other. Have the children use the cards inside the bags to make the subtraction problem shown on the sheet of paper.

5. Next, have the children rearrange the cards to make and record an add-to-check problem.

6. Allow the children time to share their results with the class. Help the children realize that every subtraction problem can be checked with addition.

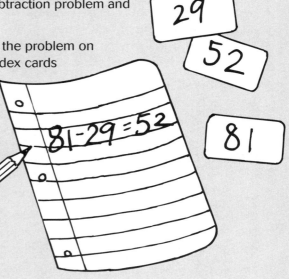

Three-Digit Block Differences

Transparency 3

1. Have the children work in pairs. Supply each pair with a photocopy of the *Place Value Mat* transparency and a collection of hundreds, tens, and ones blocks.

2. Write *637 − 165* on the chalkboard. Have each pair of children model 637 on the workmat.

3. Guide the children as they remove 5 ones from their collections and ask them to state the result (2).

4. Ask the children how they might remove 6 tens. If necessary, suggest regrouping one of the hundreds blocks as 10 tens blocks. Once children have completed the regrouping, have them remove 6 tens blocks and tell the result (7 tens, or 70).

5. The children should remove 1 hundreds block to complete the subtraction. Ask them to state the result (4 hundreds, or 400).

6. Ask a volunteer to write the answer (472) on the chalkboard. Have the children check to make sure that their workmats reflect the same number represented by their blocks.

7. Repeat with several other examples to reinforce the concept of regrouping.

Student Storytellers

This activity effectively assesses children's understanding of the meaning of addition and subtraction.

1. Give each child an index card on which an addition or a subtraction problem is written. You may use problems such as 24 + 35, 48 + 19, 90 − 25, or 72 − 28.

2. Have each child make up a story problem based on the addition or subtraction problem that he or she received.

3. Check the children's problems to make sure that they correspond to the original problem. If you have asked the children to solve the problem, check the solution.

4. When the children's work has been checked, ask volunteers to share their stories with the class and challenge their classmates to guess their problems.

Choose the Operation

In this activity, children should focus their attention on the strategy for solving the problem rather than on the actual calculations or solution.

1. Supply each child with two index cards. Have the children write an addition sign on one of their cards and a subtraction sign on the other. Encourage them to make the signs large and clear so that you can see the entire class' cards at a glance.

2. Tell a story such as the following: "Monica bowled an 85 on her first game and a 102 on the second game. How many more pins did Monica get in the second game?"

3. Ask the children to hold up the cards that show how they could solve the problem. Check to see which children chose subtraction. Ask a volunteer to explain why subtraction is the more reasonable solution strategy. If necessary, guide the children to recall that subtraction is used to compare two amounts.

4. Next, tell a story such as "Evan had 156 stickers in his collection. Then he bought a pack of 24 stickers. How many stickers does Evan have in his collection now?" After the children show their cards, ask volunteers to discuss why they chose addition.

5. Repeat for several other stories as time and interest permit.

Name _____

Fix the Mistakes

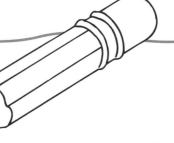

Are the subtraction facts true or false? Use blue to color the true facts. Fix the false facts. Then color them yellow. Look for a pattern.

12 − 5 = 7	15 − 8 = 7	13 − 4 = 9	16 − 8 = 8
14 − 7 = 7	10 − 5 = 3	11 − 8 = 8	10 − 8 = 2
15 − 9 = 6	14 − 6 = 6	18 − 9 = 8	17 − 9 = 9
16 − 7 = 9	15 − 7 = 7	14 − 9 = 4	11 − 9 = 3
12 − 9 = 3	10 − 7 = 3	11 − 6 = 5	13 − 7 = 6
17 − 8 = 8	16 − 9 = 6	15 − 6 = 8	14 − 8 = 6
14 − 5 = 8	13 − 5 = 9	13 − 6 = 6	12 − 7 = 5
13 − 8 = 5	13 − 9 = 7	12 − 8 = 2	12 − 6 = 6
11 − 7 = 4	10 − 4 = 6	11 − 3 = 8	10 − 3 = 7

Which letter do you see? ____

Name _____

Family Gathering

Complete each fact family.
Then write the family
members inside the triangle.

A. 5 + __7__ = 12   12 − _____ = 5

    _____ + 5 = 12   _____ − 5 = 7

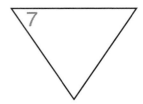

B. _____ + 8 = 15   _____ − 8 = 7

    _____ + 7 = 15   15 − _____ = 8

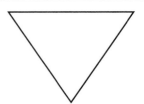

C. 6 + 7 = _____   13 − 7 = _____

    7 + _____ = 13   _____ − 6 = 7

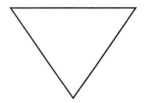

D. 9 + _____ = 16   16 − _____ = 9

    _____ + 9 = 16   _____ − 9 = 7

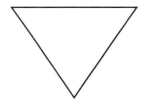

E. 8 + _____ = 14   _____ − 6 = 8

    6 + 8 = _____   14 − _____ = 6

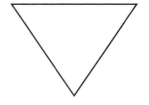

F. 4 + _____ = 13   _____ − 9 = 4

    _____ + 4 = 13   _____ − 4 = 9

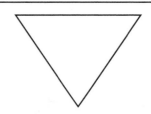

J331002 Clearly Math • Grade 2

DIFFO!

Subtract to find the difference. Shade the box with the answer. When you have five shaded boxes in a row, circle the row. You have won *DIFFO!*

A.
```
   45        57        86        30        65
 - 17      - 19      - 54      - 13      - 38
```

B.
```
   87        60        73        42        56
 - 54      - 37      - 25      - 26      - 19
```

C.
```
   83        60        57        56        56
 - 24      - 39      - 38      - 25      - 47
```

D.
```
   70        84        92        87        42
 - 21      - 39      - 51      - 86      - 29
```

D	I	F	F	O
59	38	95	31	27
33	45	48	97	13
1	94	21	17	23
93	28	16	19	41
32	49	96	9	37

Name _____

Buy and Spend

Use the *Toy Treasures* transparency to solve
each problem. Show your work.

A. Wesley had 50¢. He bought
a toy motorcycle. How much
did he have left?

_____

B. Marshall had 65¢. He bought
a large stuffed animal. How
much did he have left?

_____

C. Eve had 95¢. She bought a
travel checkers set. How
much did she have left?

_____

D. Morris had 50¢. He bought a
beaded bracelet. How much
did he have left?

_____

E. How much more does a large
stuffed animal cost than a
small stuffed animal?

_____

F. How much more does a toy
truck cost than a toy car?

_____

G. Stephanie had 75¢. She bought a toy car. Does she have enough
left to buy a toy truck? Explain.

_____

H. Suppose you have 99¢. Choose one or two items to buy. Find out
how much you will have left after you buy them.

_____

Name _____

Balloon Burst

Subtract. Color the balloon with the matching answer.

A.
  986   359   481
 − 342   − 126   − 236

B.
  624   541   674
 − 257   − 260   − 359

C.
  700   412   295   813
 − 250   − 169   − 124   − 266

D.
  908   827   579   782
 − 823   − 409   − 387   − 64

E.
  415   643   974   891
 − 209   − 539   − 382   − 587

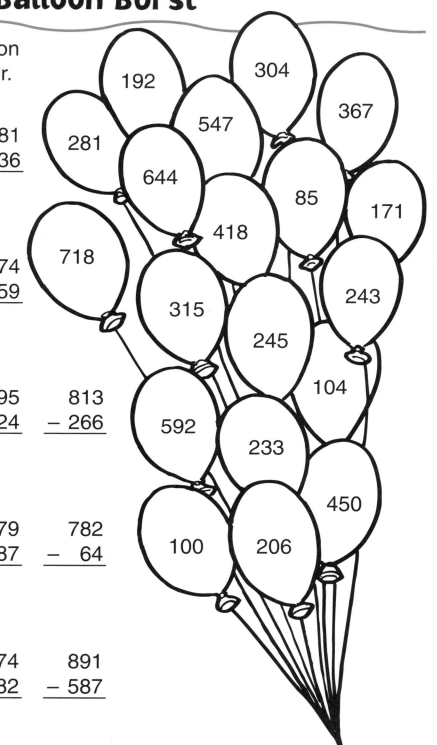

Write the number inside the balloon that is left uncolored. _____

Name _____

Living in Tiny Town

Use the *Tiny Town* transparency. Tell if you will add or subtract. Then write a number sentence and solve.

A. Marc goes through the park to get to Carrie's house. How many meters does he travel?

_____

B. Carrie took the shortcut through the park to get to the library. How many meters did she travel?

_____

C. How much farther from Marc's house is the library than the park?

_____

D. How much closer to Carrie's house is the grocery store than the park?

_____

E. Carrie can go to school two ways. She can go through the park or past the grocery store. Which way is shorter? Explain.

_____

_____

F. Marc can go to school two ways. He can go through the park or past the library. Which way is shorter? Explain.

_____

_____

Division Design

Count. Draw rings to show groups. Complete each row.

A. _____ in all   3 groups of _____

B. _____ in all   5 groups of _____

C. _____ in all   2 groups of _____

D.   _____ in all   5 groups of _____

E. _____ in all   3 groups of _____

F. _____ in all   4 groups of _____

J331002 Clearly Math • Grade 2

MONEY

Coin Names and Values

In this activity, children will review the names and values of coins.

1. Place a large collection of play coins in a paper bag. Include a variety of coins, including half-dollars, quarters, dimes, nickels, and pennies.

2. Have the children work in small groups. Invite one child in each group to reach into the bag and grab a handful of coins.

3. The children in each group should sort the handful of coins. They should name each kind of coin and arrange the collection in order from least to greatest in value.

4. Have the children find the values of the pennies, nickels, and dimes.

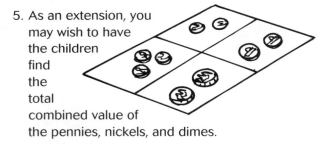

5. As an extension, you may wish to have the children find the total combined value of the pennies, nickels, and dimes.

Concentration Game

Have the children make and play their own games of concentration.

1. Supply pairs of children with sets of 20 index cards.

2. The children should draw coin collections on one card and write their values on another.

3. When ten pairs of cards have been made by each pair, have the children shuffle and place the cards facedown on a table between them.

4. The children in each pair should take turns flipping over two cards. If the collection matches the value, they take the cards. If not, they turn both cards facedown again. Play continues until all of the cards have been matched. The child in each pair with the most cards wins the round.

Mystery Collections

In this game, children use critical thinking and logical reasoning to determine which coins are in a collection.

1. Supply pairs of children with coin collections. For each collection, make sure you include pennies, nickels, dimes, quarters, and half-dollars.

2. Hide a collection of coins in a paper bag. For example, you may wish to hide 2 dimes, 2 nickels, and 1 penny.

3. Tell the children that you have a mystery collection in the bag. Disclose the number of coins and their total value. You might say, "My mystery collection has 5 coins and is worth 31¢."

4. Have the pairs of children use their coins to solve the mystery.

5. Play several rounds. If time and interest permit, have the children play the game in small groups, taking turns to make mystery collections of their own.

Toy Treasures Pay Day

In this activity, children will choose the coins that they need to pay for a toy.

1. Display the *Toy Treasures* transparency.

2. Invite the children to choose toys that they would like to buy.

3. Ask the children to draw two or more coin collections that they could use to pay for the toys. Beneath each of the collections, the children should write the numbers that show how they would count each of their coins.

4. Make sure the children's coin collections exactly match the value of the toys. Check the numbers written below the coins to assess whether the children know the value of each coin.

5. Challenge the children to tell which coin collections they would choose to pay for the items, and to explain why they chose them. (Children may choose the coin collection with the fewest coins, since it is easiest and most efficient to count.)

Coin Collection Webs

This activity focuses on children's understanding of coin values and reinforces the idea that the same value can be shown with different coin collections.

1. Distribute coin collections to small groups of children.

2. Have a child in each group place a quarter in the middle of the group's workspace. Then ask the groups to make coin collections equivalent in value to the quarter. Responses may include 2 dimes and 1 nickel, 1 dime and 3 nickels, 5 nickels, 2 dimes and 5 pennies, and so on.

3. Have each child in each group draw a web showing what they modeled with the coins.

4. Repeat the process, having children find coin collections with values equivalent to a half-dollar.

5. If children are able, extend the activity by having them create collections with values equivalent to one dollar.

J331002 Clearly Math • Grade 2

How Can You Pay?

Draw the coins needed to pay for each item.
You may draw a circle and write the name of the coin by it.

Penny   Nickel   Dime   Quarter

A.

16¢

◯ Dime

B.

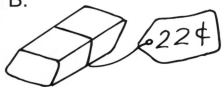

22¢

C.

29¢

D.

30¢

E.

50¢

Do You Have Enough?

Count the coins. Write the amount.
Tell whether you can buy the item. Circle *Yes* or *No.*

You want to buy	You have	Do you have enough?
A. 42¢	Total amount: _____	Yes No
B. 49¢	Total amount: _____	Yes No
C. 60¢	Total amount: _____	Yes No
D. 71¢	Total amount: _____	Yes No
E. 80¢	Total amount: _____	Yes No

F.   How did you know if you could buy an item?

_____

Exact Change

Use the *Toy Treasures* transparency. Circle the bills and coins that you need to buy each item. Use exact change.

A.

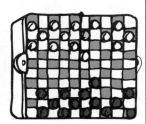 

B.

C.

D.

J331002 Clearly Math • Grade 2

Name _____

Making Change

Subtract the cost from the amount paid. Circle the coins needed.
Write a math sentence to show the amount of change.

A. A book costs 19¢. Brandon paid 25¢.

_25¢_ – _19¢_ = _____ change

B. A brush costs 17¢. Serina paid 25¢.

_____ – _____ = _____ change

C. A comb costs 13¢. Terra paid 25¢.

_____ – _____ = _____ change

D. A ribbon costs 9¢. Stephanie paid 25¢.

_____ – _____ = _____ change

E. A mirror costs 10¢. Who has enough change to buy it?

_____

TIME AND MEASUREMENT

Telling Time to the Hour

Transparency 6

This game provides a fun way to reinforce telling time to the hour and half hour.

1. Write various times to the hour and half hour in digital form on index cards. Put them in a bag or box.

2. Display the *Judy Clock* transparency.

3. Divide the class into two teams. Have each member of each team take a turn picking an index card from the bag, reading the time, and showing it on the Judy Clock.

4. Teams score 1 point for each correct answer.

5. Continue playing until all of the cards have been used.

6. Try one or more of these challenging variations:

   a. If the first answer is incorrect, the opposing team can correct it and score 1 point. The opposing team then takes its turn as it normally would and play continues.

   b. Add index cards showing time in quarter-hour or five-minute increments.

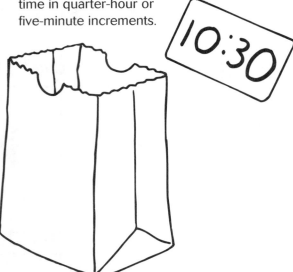

What Time Will It Be?

Transparency 6

In this activity, children will model elapsed time with the *Judy Clock* transparency.

1. Ask a volunteer to show 5:00 on the *Judy Clock* transparency.

2. Ask the children what time it will be in one hour (6:00). Invite a child to change the Judy Clock to show the new time and have the children read it aloud.

3. Ask the children what time it will be in half an hour (6:30). Invite a child to change the Judy Clock to show the new time and have the children read it aloud.

4. Repeat the procedure, varying the elapsed time in hour or half-hour increments. After each change, make sure the entire class can read the new time.

Daily School Schedule

Children will evaluate their own school schedule in this activity.

1. List on the chalkboard the time for each activity from your daily lesson plans.

2. Have the children read the times and activities aloud.

3. Have the children interpret the schedule by asking questions such as, "Will we have reading before or after math today?" "Will we have lunch before or after reading today?" "Which activity starts on the hour?" "On the half hour?" "What time is lunch?" "What time is math today?"

4. Have the children write journal entries telling what they know about the daily schedule. Children's responses should be organized in some way and include correctly written times. Specifically, children may write about the times for each activity, how long activities last, which activity lasts longest, the order of the activities, and so forth. Children may write times with words or numbers.

About How Long?

This activity helps children create their own benchmarks for length.

1. Have children work in groups. Provide each group with an inch ruler and a yardstick. Allow children several minutes to circulate around the room and measure various objects. You may suggest measuring objects such as a chalkboard eraser, a chalkboard ledge, a chair, a desk, a pencil, a book, and a stapler. Recording the lengths is optional.

2. Distribute plain white paper and crayons or colored pencils. Demonstrate how to fold the paper into four sections. Tell the children to label the sections as follows: *about 3 feet wide, about 1 foot long, about 6 inches long, about 3 inches long.*

   About 3 inches long.

3. Challenge the children to draw objects that would have the estimated lengths given in each section. Children may draw the objects that they previously measured.

4. Allow the children time to share their results within their groups and then with the class. Encourage the children to discuss and revise unreasonable estimates, if any arise.

Nonsense Metric Measurement Sentences

This activity assesses children's understanding of appropriate metric measurement tools.

1. Write a sentence such as the following on the chalkboard or overhead projector: *Rosa weighs 6 centimeters more than Nate.*

2. Ask the children to read the sentence and tell why it doesn't make sense (centimeters are not weighed). Have a volunteer change the sentence so that it's reasonable. (One possible response: *Rosa weighs 6 kilograms more than Nate.*)

3. Repeat the procedure with a sentence such as *Delinda jogged 5 liters this morning.* (Jogging isn't measured in liters; *Delinda jogged five kilometers this morning.*)

4. After one or two other examples, challenge the children to write nonsense sentences of their own. Allow the children time to share their sentences with the class.

I Spy

Children will learn about metric measurement as they play this estimation game.

1. Have pairs of children collect several classroom objects.

2. When they are finished, have the children in each pair place the objects between them on a table or the floor.

3. One child should say, "I spy something about ___ cm long. What is it?"

4. The child's partner should guess which object is being described. Players should measure the object to confirm or disprove the estimate.

5. Players should switch roles and continue to play.

Name _____

Time and Again

Write the times. Use your answers to break the code and read a special message.

A. 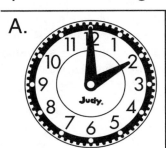	E. 	F. 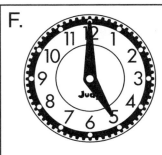	I. 
_____	_____	_____	_____

K. 	M. 	N. 	O. 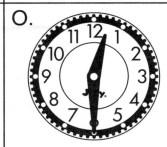
_____	_____	_____	_____

R. 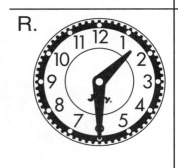	T. 	U. 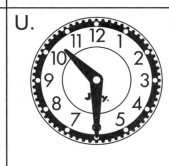	S. 
_____	_____	_____	_____

7:00	2:00	11:00	3:30	4:00	8:30	7:00	3:30

5:00	12:30	1:30	5:00	10:30	9:30

Time Match

Match.

A.

12:15

Quarter till 11

B.

11:45

Quarter past 11

C.

11:15

Quarter till 12

D.

1:15

Quarter past 12

E.

10:45

Quarter till 1

F.

1:45

Quarter past 1

G.

12:45

Quarter till 2

H.

2:15

Quarter past 2

Name _____

The Time Is Right

Does the time match the clock? Circle *Yes* or *No*.
If it doesn't match, write the correct time on the line.

A.

Yes   11:15   No

_____

B.

Yes   12:45   No

_____

C.

Yes   6:20   No

_____

D.

Yes   9:25   No

_____

E.

Yes   7:50   No

_____

F.

Yes   5:40   No

_____

G.

Yes   4:35   No

_____

H.

Yes   1:10   No

_____

I.

Yes   3:05   No

_____

Inching Along

Use an inch ruler. Measure each part of the path.
Complete the table.

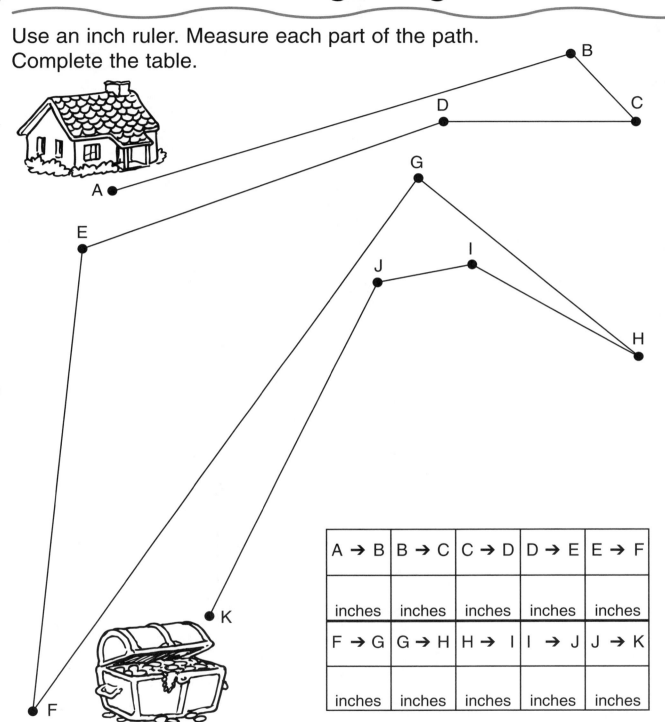

A → B	B → C	C → D	D → E	E → F
inches	inches	inches	inches	inches
F → G	G → H	H → I	I → J	J → K
inches	inches	inches	inches	inches

How can you find the distance from home to the treasure box?

_____

What is the total distance? _____

Home Beautiful

Use a centimeter ruler. Measure each line on the house. Color the lines to show the length.

15 cm orange	10 cm green	9 cm brown	5 cm red	3 cm blue

Name _____

Best Estimate

Circle the best estimate.

A.

4 pounds	4 inches
4 cups	4 feet

B.

8 cups	8 pounds
8 feet	8 quarts

C.

6 ounces	6 pounds
6 quarts	6 inches

D.

2 pounds	2 quarts
2 inches	2 yards

E.

4 gallons	4 yards
4 feet	4 tons

F.

7 ounces	7 pounds
7 inches	7 feet

Draw something that is measured in

G. inches	H. pounds	I. cups

Geometry and Fractions

Geometric Solid Collages

Children will learn to see geometric space figures all around them.

1. Have the children work in groups of four. Provide each group with magazines, scissors, glue, magic markers, and four sheets of construction paper.

2. Have the children cut out pictures of objects that represent solids such as spheres, cylinders, cubes, and rectangular prisms, and plane-shaped objects that result from the solids. For example, children may cut out pictures of soup cans and CDs as examples of cylinders and circles.

3. When the children have finished cutting, have them sort the pictures by shape.

4. Each child should choose one geometric solid shape from which to make a collage. He or she should use marker to write the name of that geometric solid on a sheet of construction paper. Children in each group should take all of their shape cutouts and arrange them to form a collage. Allow the children time to share their collages. Display if space permits.

Sides and Corners

Transparency 8

ACU

In this activity, children's understanding of fraction and geometry concepts is assessed.

1. Provide each child with a collection of real or paper pattern blocks cut from a photocopy of the *Pattern Block Design* transparency. Ask the children to classify the pattern blocks by counting the number of sides and/or corners.

2. Have each child draw a table to record the results of his or her investigation, showing each shape and indicating the number of sides and corners.

⬡	⬯	◇	△	□
6	4	4	3	4

3. Next, have the children trace each pattern block except the trapezoid and triangle three times on plain sheets of paper. For each shape, have children show how it can be divided to show two, three, and four equal parts.

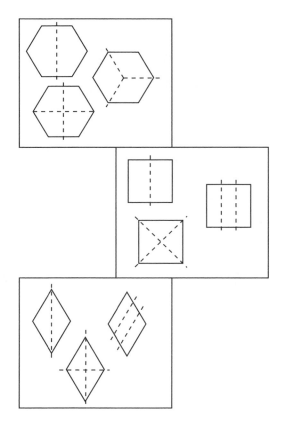

LLetter Perfect

Give each student a copy of the *Pattern Block Design* transparency for this shared learning activity.

1. Have the students cut the shapes apart.

2. Ask the students to form their initials with the pattern blocks.

3. Ask the class the following questions: "How many blocks make up your first initial?" "How many blocks are hexagons?" "How many blocks are trapezoids?" "How can we show these relationships with written numbers?" ($\frac{1}{6}$, $\frac{2}{6}$)

4. Continue to ask questions and have students write the fractions that describe the blocks they use to make their initials.

6 blocks make up the letter "R".

$\frac{1}{6}$ of the blocks are hexagons.

$\frac{2}{6}$ of the blocks are trapezoids.

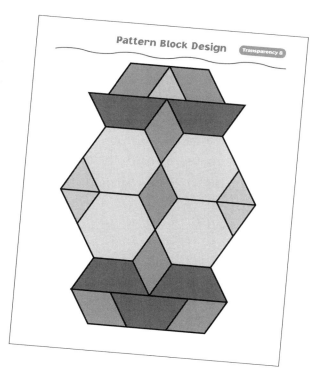

Pattern Block Design (Transparency 8)

The Same Game

In this game, children will construct congruent figures by using oral descriptions.

1. Have children work in pairs. Distribute geoboards and geobands and/or geoboard paper to each child.

2. One child in each pair secretly draws a triangle or quadrilateral on his or her geoboard.

3. The child describes the shape in terms of number of sides and corners and the length (in pegs or dots) of each side. The child's partner models or sketches the described shape on his or her geoboard.

4. Have the children compare shapes and discuss. Children switch roles and repeat the activity.

5. If time and interest permit, ask a volunteer to read his or her description to the class while another child stands at the overhead and models the shape on the geoboard.

Name _____

Letters and Words

A. Draw all of the lines of symmetry that you can.
   Write *0, 1,* or *2* on the line to tell how many you drew.

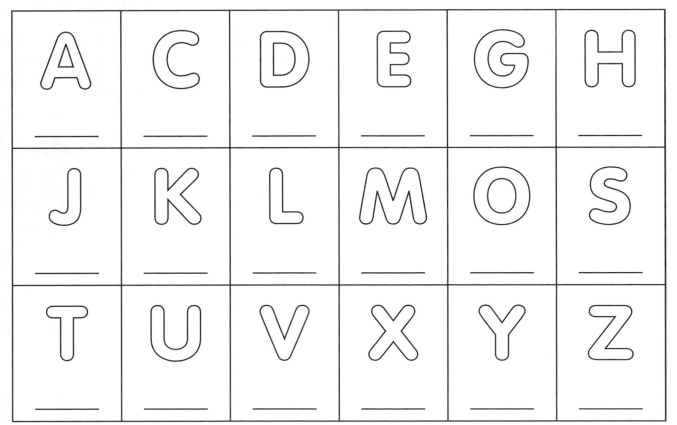

B. Write a word that has one line of symmetry.

_____

- -

_____

J331002 Clearly Math • Grade 2

All Around Tiny Town

LLook at the *Tiny Town* transparency. Find the distance around each part of Tiny Town's track. Write a number sentence.

A. What is the total distance around the track between the library, the park, and the school?

_____

B. What is the total distance around the track between the school, the cleaners, and the grocery store?

_____

C. What is the total distance around the track between the school, the diner, and the library?

_____

D. What is the total distance around the track between the park, the grocery store, and the school?

_____

E. Starting at school, Marta can walk past the cleaners and the grocery store or past the diner and the library. Which is the shorter distance? By how much? (Hint: Use answers from B and C.)

_____

F. Starting at the park, Boris can walk past the library and the school or the grocery store and the school. Which is the shorter distance? By how much? (Hint: Use answers from A and D.)

_____

G. Make a path starting at Marc's house around the school and home again. Tell the places you pass and the total distance.

_____

Pick a Part

Write the fraction for each shaded part. Write the letter from the code to answer the riddle:

What is a dime worth?

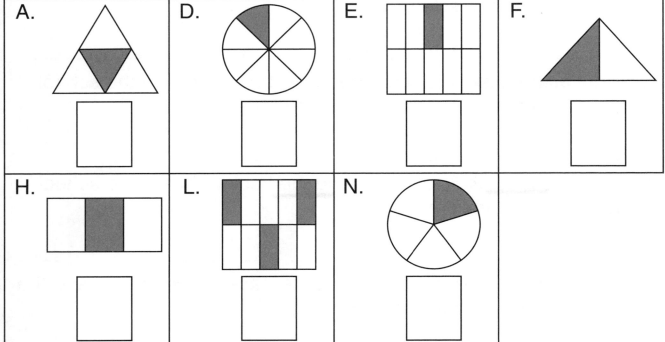

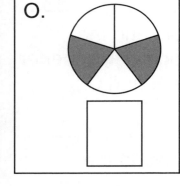

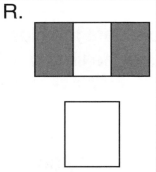

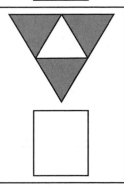

$$\frac{1}{4} \qquad \frac{3}{4} \quad \frac{1}{10} \quad \frac{1}{5} \quad \frac{3}{4} \quad \frac{1}{3} \qquad \frac{2}{5} \quad \frac{1}{2}$$

$$\frac{1}{4} \qquad \frac{1}{8} \quad \frac{2}{5} \quad \frac{3}{10} \quad \frac{3}{10} \quad \frac{1}{4} \quad \frac{2}{3}$$

J331002 Clearly Math • Grade 2

Just Name It!

What part of each name is vowels?
What part of each name is consonants?
Write the fractions. The first one has been done for you.

A. SAM	B. KAREN	C. CHUCK
$\dfrac{1}{3}$ ____ vowels $\dfrac{2}{3}$ ____ consonants	____ vowels ____ consonants	____ vowels ____ consonants
D. RUTH	E. BEA	F. CARLOS
____ vowels ____ consonants	____ vowels ____ consonants	____ vowels ____ consonants
G. MADISON	H. STEPHEN	I. BENJAMIN
____ vowels ____ consonants	____ vowels ____ consonants	____ vowels ____ consonants

J.   Write your first name. _____

What fraction, or part, is vowels? _____

What fraction, or part, is consonants? _____

DATA AND PROBABILITY

Patterns on the Judy Clock

Transparency 6

This activity provides practice with telling time and helps children identify and extend patterns.

1. Display the *Judy Clock* transparency and set the clock to 12:00.

2. Tell the children to watch the clock. Reset it to 12:30.

3. Repeat, resetting it to 1:00, then 1:30.

4. Invite volunteers to identify the pattern (the time is 30 minutes later each time) and to tell which time will come next (2:00).

5. Repeat the activity for other time increments, such as quarter hours.

Survey Says . . .

In this activity, children will record and interpret the results of a classroom survey.

1. Tell the children to think of their favorite indoor games.

2. As the children respond, record their choices on a tally chart on the chalkboard or overhead projector.

3. When all of the children have responded, ask them to display the data in a table, bar graph, or pictograph. Then ask them to describe the results. Encourage them to tell which game was most/least popular, how many children chose each game, and how the data may be used.

Exploring Probability

This fun game enables children to think about the likelihood of events.

1. Have the children work in pairs. Provide each pair with a paper bag and 6 blue cubes, 3 green cubes, and 1 yellow cube.

2. Children in each pair should take turns predicting which color cube will be picked and then drawing a cube from the bag. If the prediction is correct, the player scores a point.

3. Play should continue until each child has had 20 turns at making predictions. The child with the highest score wins the game.

4. After the games, ask the children to write about what happened. Encourage them to describe the probability of drawing a blue, green, or yellow cube in terms of certain, very likely, unlikely, or impossible. Ask them to tell who won the game and why their predictions earned them a winning score. (Children should identify blue as being very likely, green less likely, and yellow unlikely; they should acknowledge that the child who predicted "blue" more often was the most likely to win the game.)

Coin Jar

This pictograph shows the change that Mr. Garcia has in a coin jar.

Mr. Garcia's Coin Jar

Pennies	🪙 🪙 🪙 🪙 🪙 🪙 🪙 🪙 🪙 🪙
Nickels	🪙 🪙 🪙
Dimes	🪙 🪙 🪙 🪙 🪙
Quarters	🪙 🪙

Write the number that makes the sentence true.

A. Mr. Garcia has _____ quarters.

B. Mr. Garcia has _____ nickels.

C. Mr. Garcia's pennies are worth _____ .

D. Mr. Garcia's dimes are worth _____ .

E. Mr. Garcia's nickels are worth _____ .

F. There are _____ more dimes than nickels.

G. There are _____ fewer quarters than dimes.

H. Mr. Garcia has _____ coins in his coin jar.

I. Does Mr. Garcia have more than $1.00 in his coin jar? Tell how you know.

_____

_____

_____

Name _____

Get in Shape!

Look at the *Pattern Block Design* transparency.
Complete the bar graph.

Pattern Block Design

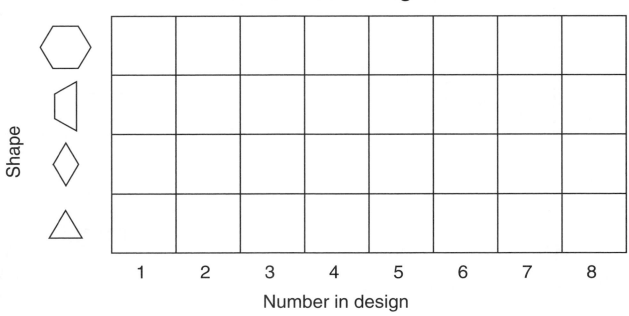

A. Write how many there are of each shape.

B. How many more ◇ than △ ? _____

C. How many more △ than ⬡ ? _____

D. Write something that you can see from reading the bar graph.

_____

_____

_____

Pattern Jumble

Use the numbers in the box to make a pattern. Describe the pattern that you made by filling in the blank and circling *more* or *less*. Use the *Number Lines* transparency to help.

A.

180 160
170
150   190

___ ___ ___ ___ ___

Each number is _____ more less.

B.

200   160
180
140   120

___ ___ ___ ___ ___

Each number is _____ more less.

C.

250   300
350
325   275

___ ___ ___ ___ ___

Each number is _____ more less.

D.

500   200
350
425   275

___ ___ ___ ___ ___

Each number is _____ more less.

E.

900   800
750
700   850

___ ___ ___ ___ ___

Each number is _____ more less.

F.

350   650
500
800   950

___ ___ ___ ___ ___

Each number is _____ more less.

G. Make up your own number pattern. Write the numbers in the pattern. Then describe the pattern in words.

_____

Answers

Page 7

Page 8

1.	65, S	2.	52, H
3.	76, E	4.	21, G
5.	91, O	6.	30, E
7.	50, S	8.	87, T
9.	41, O	10.	63, S
11.	90, W	12.	31, E
13.	41, E	14.	50, P

What does a broom do at night?
SHE GOES TO SWEEP

Page 9

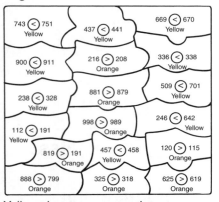

Page 10

Yellow shapes > orange shapes.

Page 11

A. 197→285→358→**532**
B. 241→405→617→**852**
C. 319→530→619→**927**
D. 456→546→555→**654**
E. 416→429→498→**501**
F. 273→295→308→**327**
G. 779→780→817→**821**
H. 511→514→520→**541**

Page 14

A.

5	2	7
3	1	4
8	3	(11)

B.

6	0	(6)
7	2	(9)
(13)	(2)	(15)

C.

4	8	(12)
3	1	(4)
(7)	(9)	(16)

D.

3	5	(8)
3	6	(9)
(6)	(11)	(17)

E.

1	9	(10)
4	3	(7)
(5)	(12)	(17)

F.

2	1	(3)
7	8	(15)
(9)	(9)	(18)

Page 15

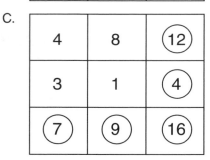

Page 16

A. 19, 20, ~~34~~, 44; 19 + 20 + 44 = 83
B. 14, ~~23~~, 25, 33; 14 + 25 + 33 = 72
C. ~~12~~, 14, 26, 28; 14 + 26 + 28 = 68
D. 12, 19, ~~37~~, 49; 12 + 19 + 49 = 80
E. 17, 28, ~~38~~, 43; 17 + 28 + 43 = 88
F. 26, 32, 35, ~~41~~; 26 + 32 + 35 = 93
G. 11, ~~13~~, 24, 35; 11 + 24 + 35 = 70
H. 19, ~~23~~, 38, 41; 19 + 38 + 41 = 98

Page 17

A. 19¢ + 25¢ = 42¢
B. 29¢ + 29¢ = 58¢
C. 38¢ + 49¢ = 87¢
D. 28¢ + 65¢ = 93¢
E. 15¢ + 15¢ + 49¢ = 79¢
F. 28¢ + 29¢ + 38¢ = 95¢
G. Yes. 56¢ + 15¢ = 71¢; 71¢ > 65¢
H. No. 25¢ + 12¢ = 37¢; 37¢ < 38¢
I. Responses will vary.

Page 18

A. 700, 589, 764, 229, 938
B. 592, 586, 935, 494, 732
C. 919, 634, 554, 754, 389
D. 828, 715, 516, 714, 752

700	123	589	456	754	721	938
494	189	919	314	752	592	935
516	517	186	442	715	487	634
554	201	732	322	714	101	828
764	897	586	789	389	915	229

The secret word: HI

Page 19

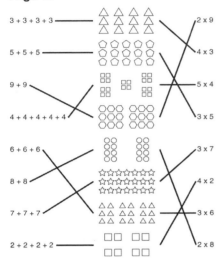

Page 23

12 − 5 = 7	15 − 8 = 7	13 − 4 = 9	16 − 8 = 8
14 − 7 = 7	10 − 5 = X = 5	11 − 8 = X = 3	10 − 8 = 2
15 − 9 = 6	14 − 6 = X = 8	18 − 9 = X = 9	17 − 9 = X = 8
16 − 7 = 9	15 − 7 = X = 8	14 − 9 = X = 5	11 − 9 = X = 2
12 − 9 = 3	10 − 7 = 3	11 − 6 = 5	13 − 7 = 6
17 − 8 = X = 9	16 − 9 = X = 7	15 − 6 = X = 9	14 − 8 = 6
14 − 5 = X = 9	13 − 5 = X = 8	13 − 6 = X = 7	12 − 7 = 5
13 − 8 = 5	13 − 9 = X = 4	12 − 8 = X = 4	12 − 6 = 6
11 − 7 = 4	10 − 4 = 6	11 − 3 = 8	10 − 3 = 7

Which letter do you see? The letter *S.*

Page 24

A. 5 + 7 = 12, 12 − 7 = 5
   7 + 5 = 12, 12 − 5 = 7
   Family members: 5, 7, 12
B. 7 + 8 = 15, 15 − 8 = 7
   8 + 7 = 15, 15 − 7 = 8
   Family members: 7, 8, 15
C. 6 + 7 = 13, 13 − 7 = 6
   7 + 6 = 13, 13 − 6 = 7
   Family members: 6, 7, 13
D. 9 + 7 = 16, 16 − 7 = 9
   7 + 9 = 16, 16 − 9 = 7
   Family members: 7, 9, 16
E. 8 + 6 = 14, 14 − 6 = 8
   6 + 8 = 14, 14 − 8 = 6
   Family members: 6, 8, 14
F. 4 + 9 = 13, 13 − 9 = 4
   9 + 4 = 13, 13 − 4 = 9
   Family members: 4, 9, 13

Page 25

A. 28, 38, 32, 17, 27
B. 33, 23, 48, 16, 37
C. 59, 21, 19, 31, 9
D. 49, 45, 41, 1, 13

D	I	F	F	O
59	38	95	31	27
33	45	48	97	13
1	94	21	17	23
93	28	16	19	41
32	49	96	9	37

Page 26

A. 50¢ − 29¢ = 21¢
B. 65¢ − 65¢ = 0¢
C. 95¢ − 85¢ = 10¢
D. 50¢ − 17¢ = 33¢
E. 65¢ − 28¢ = 37¢
F. 49¢ − 38¢ = 11¢
G. No. 75¢ − 38¢ = 37¢; 37¢ is not enough to buy a truck.
H. Responses will vary.

Page 27

A. 644, 233, 245
B. 367, 281, 315
C. 450, 243, 171, 547
D. 85, 418, 192, 718
E. 206, 104, 592, 304
The number inside the balloon left uncolored: 100

Page 28

A. Add; 136 + 71 = 207m
B. Add; 136 + 40 = 176m
C. Subtract; 128 − 71 = 57m
D. Subtract; 136 − 125 = 11m
E. Going past the grocery store (235m) is shorter than going through the park (286m).
F. Going through the park (221m) is shorter than passing the library (228m).

Page 29

A. 12 in all; 3 groups of 4
B. 15 in all; 5 groups of 3
C. 16 in all; 2 groups of 8
D. 20 in all; 5 groups of 4
E. 21 in all; 3 groups of 7
F. 24 in all; 4 groups of 6

Page 32

Answers will vary.

Page 33

A. Total amount: 36¢; No
B. Total amount: 50¢; Yes
C. Total amount: 60¢; Yes
D. Total amount: 75¢; Yes
E. Total amount: 76¢; No
F. Answers will vary.

Page 34

A. 1 half-dollar, 1 quarter, 1 dime
B. 1 dollar, 1 quarter, 1 dime
C. 1 dollar, 1 dime, 1 nickel, 4 pennies
D. 1 dollar, 2 quarters, 4 dimes

Page 35

A. 1 penny, 1 nickel; 6¢ change
B. 3 pennies, 1 nickel; 8 ¢ change
C. 2 pennies, 1 dime; 12¢ change
D. 1 penny, 1 nickel, 1 dime; 16¢ change
E. Terra and Stephanie.

Page 38

A.	2:00	E.	3:30
F.	5:00	I.	8:30
K.	11:00	M.	7:00
N.	9:30	O.	12:30
R.	1:30	T.	4:00
U.	10:30	S.	6:00

The secret message: MAKE TIME FOR FUN

Page 39

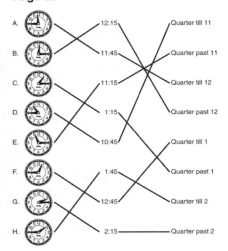

Page 40

A.	No; 10:15	B.	Yes
C.	No; 7:20	D.	Yes
E.	No; 8:50	F.	No; 4:40
G.	No; 3:35	H.	Yes
I.	Yes		

Page 41

A→B = 5 inches		B→C = 1 inch
C→D = 2 inches		D→E = 4 inches
E→F = 5 inches		F→G = 7 inches
G→H = 3 inches		H→I = 2 inches
I→J = 1 inch		J→K = 4 inches

To find the distance from home to the treasure box, add.

Total distance: 34 inches

Page 42

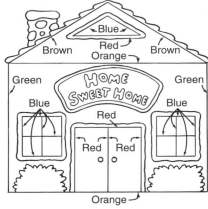

Page 43

A.	4 pounds	B.	8 quarts
C.	6 pounds	D.	2 quarts
E.	4 feet	F.	7 inches
G.	Drawings will vary.		
H.	Drawings will vary.		
I.	Drawings will vary.		

Page 46

1	1	1	1	0	2
0	1	0	1	2	0
1	1	1	2	1	0

B. Responses will vary.

Page 47

A. $40 + 150 + 100 = 290m$
B. $78 + 98 + 110 = 286m$
C. $85 + 96 + 100 = 281m$
D. $142 + 110 + 150 = 402m$
E. Passing the cleaners and grocery
   store is 5 meters shorter.
F. Passing the library and the
   school is 112 meters shorter.
G. Answers will vary.

Page 48

A.	$1/4$	D.	$1/8$
E.	$1/10$	F.	$1/2$
H.	$1/3$	L.	$3/10$
N.	$1/5$	O.	$2/5$
R.	$2/3$	T.	$3/4$

What is a dime worth? A TENTH OF A DOLLAR

Page 49

A. $1/3$ vowels, $2/3$ consonants
B. $2/5$ vowels, $3/5$ consonants
C. $1/5$ vowels, $4/5$ consonants
D. $1/4$ vowels, $3/4$ consonants
E. $2/3$ vowels, $1/3$ consonants
F. $2/6$ vowels, $4/6$ consonants
G. $3/7$ vowels, $4/7$ consonants
H. $2/7$ vowels, $5/7$ consonants
I. $3/8$ vowels, $5/8$ consonants
J. Responses will vary.

Page 51

A.	2 quarters	B.	3 nickels
C.	10¢	D.	50¢
E.	15¢		

F. 2 more dimes than nickels
G. 3 fewer quarters than dimes
H. 20 coins are in the jar
I. Yes; explanations will vary.

Page 52

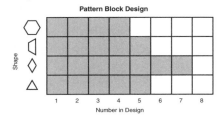

A. 4 hexagons, 5 trapezoids,
   7 rhombi, 5 triangles
B. There are 2 more rhombi than
   triangles.
C. There is one more triangle
   than there are hexagons.
D. Answers will vary.

Page 53

A. Each number is 10 (more or less)
B. Each number is 20 (more or less)
C. Each number is 25 (more or less)
D. Each number is 75 (more or less)
E. Each number is 50 (more or less)
F. Each number is 150 (more or less)
G. Answers will vary.